Take your time

Live in the moment

Don't rush

Be more present

Find pleasure in the small things

Take time for yourself

Relax

Sleep is important

Enjoy life

Let things go

Drink more water

Exercise often

Hang out with friends and family

Be grateful

Believe in yourself

Smile often

Don't compare yourself to others

Stay calm

Be kind to others

Have fun

www.ingramcontent.com/pod-product-compliance
Lightning Source LLC
Chambersburg PA
CBHW040418100526
44588CB00022B/2872